SCOTTISH
COUNTRY
DANCING

Isobel E. Williams

Chambers

CHAMBERS
An imprint of Larousse plc
43–45 Annandale Street
Edinburgh EH7 4AZ

First published by Chambers 1991
Reprinted 1993, 1994

A CIP catalogue record for this book is
available from the British Library

ISBN 0 550 20063 0

Diagrams by John Haxby
© Larousse plc
Cover design by John Marshall

Typeset by Bookworm Typesetting Ltd, Edinburgh
Printed in Singapore by
Singapore National Printers Ltd

Contents

JIGS

STRATHSPEYS

Introduction

A Short History of Country Dancing in Scotland

An Irishman watching children doing Scottish country dancing was once heard to remark that he had never seen children 'so handy with their feet'. Not only children, but almost all Scots are great dancers, most of them having learned one or two dances at school. They have probably danced Strip the Willow or the Gay Gordons at a wedding reception or a Hogmanay party and almost everyone knows the tune of the Dashing White Sergeant. The Scots have good tunes and their traditional dances are great fun, not least when differences of opinion arise as to how to do them. They seem to take their elegant strathspeys and waltzes and strenuous jigs and reels more or less for granted; for they are so used to them just being there . . . a bit like heather, tartan and whisky.

What is known today as Scottish country dancing is, however, actually a mixture of native dances which go back a long way and foreign dances which have been added to them and have influenced them over the centuries. Elements still remain today of ritual dances performed by the earliest inhabitants of Scotland to ensure fertility or a good hunt. Many circle dances may hark back to the worship of pagan gods where the movement of the circle is usually clockwise, in the direction of the sun, for good luck. Bridal reels, either foursomes performed by the bride and groom with the bridesmaid and best man, or sixsomes to include an older married couple, are the remains of old fertility rites, danced to ensure a happy and fruitful marriage. Together with these native peasant dances go foreign court dances, some of which may have been brought to Scotland as early as the eleventh century.

In 1070, Margaret, the English princess who married Malcolm Canmore, introduced foreigners from England and abroad into the Scottish court. They brought with them instruments and music from their own countries and it is very likely that they brought their dances too. At the start of the twelfth century, one of the sons of Margaret and Malcolm, David I, married a Norman wife and introduced Norman manners and dances to the court, and the Auld Alliance, formalized in 1295, cemented the ties with France. With French and Scots troops serving together over the centuries, music and dance were undoubtedly influences in both countries among the people as well as at the courts.

At the start of the fifteenth century, dances which had originated in the French countryside and were gaining popularity throughout most of Western Europe became popular at the Scottish court. Called *basse*, meaning

2

'low' or 'peasant' dances, these continued to be favourite dances into the sixteenth century. Mary of Guise, the French wife of James V, surrounded herself with French retainers and things French, including dances, and Mary Queen of Scots continued to dance when she came from the French court at Versailles to Holyrood Palace in 1561, despite an attempt to ban dancing by the Church in Scotland at this time. Records of punishment meted out to those dancing on a Sunday or dancing in the kirkyard at this period show that the common people continued to dance as well . . . in spite of John Knox.

Though the people had always copied the nobles they had also kept up their own reels and circle dances. The Scottish court, on the other hand, had been restricted to couples dancing round the room. However, in the second half of the sixteenth century, the English court had adopted a form of dance in which couples took their places opposite each other in lines down the room. Called 'country' dance, this type of dancing was much more sociable, with couples dancing with other couples and not just by themselves. This was what James I and VI was introduced to when he moved his court from Edinburgh to London in 1603.

Controversy abounds as to why country dance is so called. Some historians suggest that it comes from the word *contrapassi*, a sort of figure dance mentioned in books of Italian dancing masters. Some say it comes from the French *contre*, meaning 'opposite', because couples dance opposite each other, whereas others say that the French took the English word 'country' and changed it to *contre*. Yet another theory is that these dances were first performed at court masques and danced in a country setting as a sort of pastoral dance.

Whatever the origin of the name, it was to take over fifty years for 'country' dance to reach Scotland. In 1649 the General Assembly of the Church of Scotland had passed an Act prohibiting 'promiscuous dancing', resulting in dancing being severely curtailed. Though it was undoubtedly still enjoyed, dancing was a clandestine affair which the Church equated with sexual permissiveness. Happily, a visit by the Duke and Duchess of York, when they stayed in Holyrood Palace from 1680 to 1682, revived dancing once again, and introduced 'new' dances, including the country dance.

Scottish country dancing has never been danced by the upper classes of society alone, so it was not long before all levels of Edinburgh society were doing the new dances.

At the start of the eighteenth century, regular public dances were taking place in Edinburgh at the West Bow Assembly. Modelled on the Assemblies organized by Beau Nash in Bath, the profits from them went to various charities, including the Edinburgh Royal Infirmary, helping to find favour for the dances even with the Kirk! Similar public dances followed in Leith, Glasgow, Haddington, Perth, Inverness and Aberdeen, with a Master of Ceremonies calling out the dances. If dances were well known, he only called out the title, but new or unfamiliar dances were talked through, much in the style of a 'caller' at a dance today. In the 1760s a new type of slow reel, the strathspey, appeared on the dance programmes at the Assemblies and caught on very quickly.

Perhaps what helped to fix country dancing so firmly among other Scottish traditions was the visit of George IV organized by Sir Walter Scott in 1822. Filling Edinburgh with Highland chiefs, kilts, tartanalia and other manifestations of 'fake'-lore, the visit was a round of banquets and balls in which Scottish dancing was performed with zeal. George IV threw himself wholeheartedly into the whole thing, going so far as to don the kilt. As one Edinburgh matron put it when seeing his fat figure swathed in tartan, 'With his stay being so short, the more we see of him the better.'

The revived enthusiasm for Scottish dancing was such that when Queen Victoria and Prince Albert first came to Scotland in 1842 they were treated to displays of reels wherever they went. Dances became a feature of royal life at Balmoral, rebuilt in 1855, and continued to be popular throughout the country until the end of the century. New influences continued to come in, notably in the form of Swedish dances, in which one couple face another couple and pass on at the end of each dance sequence to face a new couple. The Dashing White Sergeant is a good example of this. The Waltz Country Dance, combining the popular Viennese 'Walzer' with the 'Swedish' progression, had also appeared by the end of the nineteenth century, as had various other forms of progression like Poussette and Allemande.

By the beginning of this century, however, what had been a growing and developing tradition enjoyed by everyone in Scotland looked as if it was going to be overwhelmed by the influence of European ballroom dancing and American dances like the foxtrot and tango; it seemed destined to die out. Far from it. Scottish dances have been, and still are, danced and enjoyed . . . not just by Scots but by people of all ages and nationalities all over the world.

The Royal Scottish Country Dance Society, formed as the Scottish Country Dance Society in Glasgow in 1923 to preserve what was thought to be a dying tradition, now has over 28 000 members all over the world. As well as documenting dances and training teachers, the RSCDS organizes dances in Scotland and abroad.

Apart from these formal gatherings, informal dances and ceilidhs take place regularly wherever a few Scots meet, for dancing is the kind of sociable entertainment that can be enjoyed anywhere and at any time. No special equipment is necessary, for as long as someone can whistle or chant the music, that is all that is needed. Perhaps the best example that Scottish country dancing is adaptable to any situation is the dance the Reel of the 51st Division, composed and danced by the officers and men of the 51st while serving as prisoners of war in Germany in 1940.

This book supplies instructions for dancers in an informal setting and it is hoped that it will encourage readers to enjoy the dance.

Dress

The Kilt

The version of the kilt which we have today is a far cry from the original blanket, dyed with natural pigments, which the Highlanders wrapped around themselves a few centuries ago. Called in Gaelic a *féileadh* this was the essential item of dress for the Scottish Highlanders before it was banned in 1746. It was, in effect, a sort of blanket – a plaid which was pinned over the chest with a piece of bone or wood and tied round the middle with a leather belt. Most of the part which hung down from the belt was pleated but about a yard either side was left unpleated. When the wearers were on the move it was easy enough to unwrap the plaid at night and use it as a cover.

The material used for plaids was woven in various coloured checks and stripes, and the material was called plaiding. The dyes for the colours came from local plants and people from different areas wore different coloured plaids depending on the varieties of plants in their region. Nowadays the many checked patterns (setts) represent the tartans of various clans.

In 1746 an Act for the 'Abolition and Proscriptiion of the Highland dress' was passed and the Highlanders were forced into 'trews' (trousers). The Act was repealed in 1782, though the kilt was still regarded as something to be worn by the Highland peasants.

Today, it is an item of dress more associated with Lowlanders. The visit of George IV to Edinburgh in 1822, for which Sir Walter Scott set up a Highland pantomime with 'Geordie' himself as the kilted star, started off the trend among the upper classes for the garment. This fashion was continued during the Romantic period and reinforced by Queen Victoria and her husband Albert who had a castle built at Balmoral where they could enjoy painting and walking. The kilt became an elegant item of dress, which nowadays can still be seen adorning royal posteriors.

The kilt should not go below the knee-cap and should

not droop at the back. To test if the kilt is the proper length, kneel down and get someone to check that the kilt just brushes the ground. If it drags on the ground it is too long, if it is more than a centimetre (half an inch) above the ground it is too short. The stockings or hose should not be too long – 'choking the knees' – and should have a good turnover of about ten centimetres (four inches). Different types of jacket can be worn.

Women's Dress

For a formal dance, women wear either a long or calf-length white dress with a tartan sash. This is what was earlier worn as a plaid or shawl by the Highland women. The tartan can be either the wearer's clan tartan, or, if she has married out of her clan, her husband's. Made of some sort of light material, it is about sixty centimetres (two feet) wide. It should be long enough to allow a good drape when it is pinned on and have two fringes of about thirty centimetres (twelve inches). In general it is worn over the left shoulder, across the breast to the waist and across the back to the left shoulder where it is pinned on with a brooch, so that the fringes hang down back and front. Another common way to wear the sash is simply to double it and pin it to the left shoulder so that it hangs free at the back.

While a dress for a formal Scottish country dance can be worn on other occasions, many men do not want to go to the expense of buying a full Highland outfit to use only once, so simply hire their outfits. You do not have to dress up to enjoy the dances, however, as most Scottish country dance evenings are informal with the dancers dressed in everyday clothes.

Both men and women should wear soft shoes.

Etiquette

Organized dances, whether arranged by a country dance society to celebrate a special anniversary or by private individuals for a wedding reception or similar function, usually have a programme of dances made up by a Master of Ceremonies. He announces the dances and, if they are complicated, walks the dancers through them beforehand.

Dances are performed in 'sets', lines or circles of couples. Unless otherwise stated a set consists of a minimum of four couples and a maximum of six couples, the women with their right hand to the top of the room, men with their left hand to the top of the room.

Men	Women	
1	1	Top
2	2	
3	3	
4	4	
5	5	
6	6	Bottom

All sets perform the same routine simultaneously. The first couple of each set start off the dance by dancing with couples two and three. When the routine is finished, the first couple have moved down one place and perform the routine again with couples three and four and then with couples four and five. By this time, the second couple are at the top of the set. They then start to dance with couples three and four to progress down the set as the first couple have done before them. Every couple dances the routine, progressing down the set until the first couple are back in their original position. A good band leader, who has been keeping his eye on the set nearest to the band, finishes the dance at this point.

It goes without saying that dancers should hold themselves straight (but not stiff) and hold their heads up when dancing, aiming for an elegant, flowing movement. 'Louping aboot' (bouncing and jumping about all over the place) is not considered good form by

8

those who appreciate that Scottish country dancing is ballroom dancing and not a war dance.

On the other hand, 'hooching' or shouting out while dancing is quite acceptable. The noise is made by singing a very long monotonous 'eeeee' followed by a shout of 'yeuch'. Although the Scots may drink a lot of whisky at a good dance, the 'morning after' symptoms are more often tender feet and a sore throat than a hangover.

There are certain basic rules which should be followed regarding sets and the preliminaries to the dance.

1   Do not form a set until the Master of Ceremonies has announced the dance.

2   Always join a set at the end of the line.

3   Once you are in a set, do not leave it until the dance is finished.

4   Do not look about, talk to your neighbour or otherwise cause a disturbance if you are not dancing. Stand quietly in your position and watch the dancing couples.

5   Look at the person you are dancing with.

6   Each dance begins and ends with a bow from the men and a curtsey from the women.

Hands

When making a curtsey or a bow or when dancing Pas de Basque (see under **Basic Steps**) women usually hold the skirt of their dress out to the side a little just below hip level. Men either make fists and place their hands on their hips or hold both arms above their heads in imitation of a stag's antlers. Men often put their arms like this when dancing in the middle of a circle or doing a reel.

When crossing over, dancing in line or in a circle, hands are given at shoulder height. When dancers turn each other, various hand holds can be used. For example, both arms crossed and both hands joined; both arms crossed and both wrists grasped; arms linked at the elbow or forearms grasped. In all cases the men's hands are palm upwards, the women's hands palm downwards. Some men favour a crossed forearms grip, with the right forearms in contact and the two left hands holding each over the top as this gives them more power to swing their partner round. However, this often results in the turn going out of control and sometimes leads to accidents.

Basic Steps, Formations and Progressions

A Note For Beginners

Scottish country dancing is made up of basic steps, formations and progressions explained here in order of difficulty. Once the dancer has mastered these, there will be no trouble in following the instructions for the dances.

The basic steps and movements have to be learned and then used in the dances as they are needed. Practise each movement singly first, then walk through the dance several times. Dance the complete dance only when the basic patterns of formations and progressions have been grasped.

Notation

Describing any kind of dance with words alone is not the ideal method of teaching and beginners may feel rather overwhelmed by some of the instructions. As with learning any subject it is important to take things slowly and, most of all, to practise.

The dances are described in simple words which include instructions for specific formations or progressions. Diagrams are used when necessary. In the diagrams in this book, the dancers are depicted by a triangle topped with a circle, the dancer's head indicating the direction in which the dancer is facing. Black triangles represent men, open triangles represent women. The numbers beside the triangles refer to the dancer's number in the set.

Man

Woman

Because the dance steps should fit the music, with formations beginning and ending at the proper place so that the dance flows evenly, the number of music bars have been included to the left of each formation. All steps and progressions are started with the right foot, with exception of the slip step and hands round formation.

Slip Step

This is the simplest step in Scottish country dancing, done by taking a step sideways on the toes of the left foot, then bringing the right foot up to the left so that the heels meet. The toes of both feet should be turned out slightly. The slip step is used for dancing circles in reels and jigs.

Pas de Basque or Setting Step

This is *the* basic step in Scottish country dancing. It is very simple and is performed as follows:

1   Make a small spring on to the right foot.
2   Bring the left foot in front so that the ball of the left foot is almost in contact with the instep of the right foot and transfer the weight on to the left foot.
3   Transfer weight back on to the right foot.
4   Repeat with left foot by springing on to the left foot, bringing the right foot in front. It may help to count out "and, one, two, three, and, one, two, three' while learning how to perform this step.

Travelling Step

This step should be used when any distance is to be covered, for example, when a couple have to dance up or down a set. The travelling step has the same rhythm as Pas de Basque and can be practised by counting 'one, two, three, and, one, two, three' but, depending on the speed of the dance, it is done either quickly (reel time) or slowly (strathspey). Whatever speed it is danced at, it should be done as smoothly as possible without the dancer appearing to want to jump up to the ceiling. It is done as follows:

1   Take one step forward with the right foot (the weight should be on the right foot and on the toe of the left foot).

2   Bring the left foot up behind the right foot.

3   Take a small step forward with the right foot and hop bringing the left foot forward to continue:

1   Take one step forward with the left foot.

2   Bring the right foot up behind the left foot.

3   Take a small step forward with the left foot and hop . . .

It is necessary to note here that the travelling step described above is not taught by the Royal Scottish Country Dance Society as it is considered somewhat inelegant. However, it has been included because it is the easiest way to do a travelling step and because it is the step most popular among Scots dancers.

Hands Round

Circles can be danced 'four hands round', i.e. with four dancers, 'five hands round', with five dancers, 'six hands round', with six dancers and so on with dancers joining hands in a circle and dancing round in a clockwise direction for eight steps. The hands are held at shoulder level as this helps to control the circle more easily. If the circle is to be danced back in the other direction, it is necessary to slow down on the eighth step ready to start dancing to the right.

Advance and Retire

This formation can be danced across the set or round the room with two or three dancers. Holding hands at shoulder level, dance towards opposite dancers and then dance backwards to original position using short travelling steps. It is important that all the steps are equal, with the two steps backwards the same length as the two steps forwards.

Casting Off

This is a method of moving up or down the outside of the set on the dancer's own side.

The woman turns to her right and, using a travelling step, dances down the outside of the set. The man does the same on his side, turning to his left.

Promenade

Couples join right and left hands together, the woman on the man's right, so that their arms are crossed in front. The first couple swing out to the right on the women's side of the set with the second and third couples following. They dance across and down the left-hand side of the set to where the fourth couple are standing before turning back to return to their original starting positions.

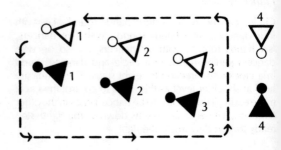

Right Hands Across
Left Hands Across

The formation looks like a wheel with the arms extended to form the spokes and the hands in the centre forming the hub. Dancers give each other their right or left hand, depending on the instructions in the dance. The first man takes the hand of the second woman and the second man takes the hand of the first woman. With the first woman's hand on top, all four hands are held together in the centre of the wheel and the dancers dance round for four steps.

Grand Chain

Danced round in a circle using a travelling step and giving right and left hands alternately. Dancers start by facing their partners and giving them their right hands. The women go in a clockwise direction, the men anti-clockwise. All the dancers go round the circle once to end up in their original positions.

Ladies' Chain

Two couples do this. The women should be standing at their partner's right side when the reel begins and ends.

1   Both women give each other the right hand and cross over to the opposite man's place while the men dance into their partner's position.

2   The first woman gives her left hand to the second man and the second woman gives her left hand to the first man.

3   All half turn with two steps, finishing with the woman on the man's right, ready to repeat the movement back to her original place. Use eight travelling steps.

Allemande

This is a way to change places.

Couples, the woman on the man's right, hold each other as follows: just as the Allemande is about to start, the man takes his partner's right hand in his right hand and her left hand in his left hand, so that their arms are crossed in front of them. He immediately lifts his partner's right arm over her head to a position just above her right shoulder. The man keeps his partner's left hand in his left hand at hip level so that he can lead her through the movement as follows:

> First couple move from the middle of the set and turn out in an arc to the right. They dance round to the left to the second couple's position. Second couple follow at the same time, dancing into first couple's position. Use eight travelling steps.

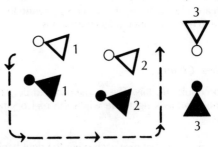

Poussette

Another way for couples to change places, the first couple moving down the set, the second couple moving up the set. Pas de Basque step is used throughout, using eight steps.

The word 'Poussette' comes from the French verb *pousser* – to push. The men should move their partner firmly but gently with the hands only. This can only be done with the hands joined at shoulder level and the elbows tucked in at the sides.

The women starting off with the right foot, the men

with the left, two couples change places in a square formation as follows:

> Holding both hands, the leading man gently pulls his partner towards him so that they move out to the man's side; the second couple move out on the woman's side, the man, in this case, pushing his partner gently. All make a quarter turn to the right to come into line with the dancers who are not doing Poussette. The men should now have their backs to the top of the set. The first couple take a step downwards, the second couple take a step upwards and turn to the right once again, the men pushing or pulling their partners as necessary. The men now have their backs to the women's side of the set. Both couples take a step to the centre and make a half turn to their own sides of the set. With the last two steps both couples move back into line and are now in each other's places.

Reel of Three

Eight travelling steps are needed for this formation which makes a perfect figure eight. Three dancers each trace out an eight, dancing either across the set, or up and down the set, with the main dancer passing his or her opposite number with the right shoulder unless otherwise stated. It can be learned easily by walking through it as follows:

Across the set, dancers stand in Reel of Three position as shown, in this example, two women and one man.

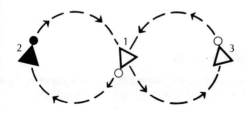

1   The first woman faces the second man whom she passes with her right shoulder.

2   At the same time, the second woman steps out to her right ready to pass the second man with her left shoulder.

3   Following the shape of a figure eight, the first woman, after having danced round the loop of the figure, passes the second woman with her left shoulder, dances the second loop of the eight and returns to her place.

Reel of Four

Two couples dance this, basically a figure of eight with a loop in the middle. It begins either with the two men standing back to back in the middle of the set between the two women or with the first couple standing back to back in the middle of the set between the other couple.

It is started by passing the dancer opposite either on the right or the left as indicated in the individual dance descriptions.

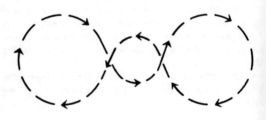

Rights and Lefts

Two couples dance round the form of a square to return to their original places in eight travelling steps.

1   Both couples give right hands to their partners and pass across the set.

2 Both couples move up or down the set, giving left hands to the same sex.

3 Giving right hands to their partners both couples pass across the set again.

4 Giving left hands to the same sex all dancers finish in their original positions. Half Rights and Lefts is as above but with dancers only moving two places.

Corners

Corners are an important formation in many dances. The dancing couple each have two corners, which form the corners of a square, and the couple are always diagonally back to back across the set when dancing with corners. The woman's first corner is the second man while the man's first corner is the third woman. Each turns to the left and the woman's second corner is the third man, and the man's is the second woman.

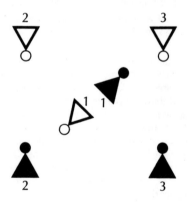

Set To and Turn Corners

This formation is often found in reels and strathspeys. It goes as follows:

1 First man sets to his 'first corner' (third woman) who sets to him.

2   Joining both hands he turns her right round to leave her in her place while he ends up facing his 'second corner' (second woman) to repeat the above with her, finishing between the second and third women.

3   At the same time the first woman is dancing the same movements with her 'corners', the second and third men.

Double Triangles

The first couple stand back to back in the middle of the set as closely as possible. They face their own sides of the dance and are, in effect, looking out of the set. The second couple is at the top of the set.

The first couple join hands with the second and third couples as follows:

1   The first man gives his right hand to the second man and his left hand to the third man.

2   The first woman gives her right hand to the third woman and her left hand to the second woman.

The formation should make the shape of the St Andrew's cross. To ensure this, it is important that the first couple stand very closely back to back. The second and third couples must be near enough to the first couple to form the shape of the cross without pulling them away from each other. Keep arms straight.

All dancers Pas de Basque and drop hands. Then, keeping closely back to back, the first couple turn right about with two steps so that they are facing the opposite sides of the set. They join hands as before and set again. Dropping hands again, the first couple turn right about into second place on their own sides of the set. This is done with two springy setting steps.

This formation is incorporated in the dance Waverley.

DANCES

REELS

Admiral Nelson

A Scottish country dance dedicated to an English admiral may seem rather strange. However, Horatio Nelson (1758–1805) was a much respected naval commander. The people of Edinburgh erected a monument to him in 1807 and this dance may have been devised at the same time.

Music: *Admiral Nelson*

Description
A longways set

8   1st and 2nd couples dance four hands round and back.

8   1st woman casts off, dancing down the outside of the set on her own side. 1st man follows and both dance round 2nd couple to finish in their original positions.

8   Repeat the last 8 bars, this time with 1st man casting off on his side and his partner following.

8   1st and 2nd couples dance Rights and Lefts. 3rd and 4th couples dance Rights and Lefts at the same time.

8   Six hands round and back.

8   1st and 2nd couples Allemande. 1st couple are now between 2nd and 3rd couples.

8   All four couples dance the Grand Chain, couples 2 and 4 dancing across the set, couples 1 and 3 up and down, continuing round until they are back in their original positions.

8   1st couple dance together up to the top, where they divide and cast off to the bottom of the set. All the other couples move up.
Repeat with a new top couple.

Bonnie Geordie's Wig

Music: *Any good reel*

Description
A longways set

4   1st and 2nd couples set twice.

4   Right hands across.

8   As first 8 bars, but with left hands across.

8   1st man dances across to 2nd woman, passing her on her left, then dances round behind 2nd man, passing him on his left. At the same time, 1st woman dances across to 2nd man, passing him on his right, then dances round behind 2nd woman, passing her on her right. 1st couple are now between 2nd and 3rd couples.

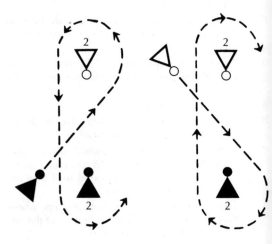

8   1st and 2nd couples Rights and Lefts.
    1st couple repeat with next couple.
    A new top couple begin on every second repetition until everyone has danced twice.

Brechin Fancy

The royal burgh of Brechin in Angus stands on the South Esk.

Music: *Any good reel*

Description
A longways set

8 1st couple dance down the middle of the set and up again.

4 1st woman turns 2nd man with the right hand. At the same time 1st man turns 2nd woman with the right hand. 1st couple return to their original positions, the woman crossing in front of her partner.

4 1st woman turns 2nd man with the left hand. At the same time 1st man turns 2nd woman with the left hand. Both couples finish ready for a Reel of Four. 1st couple are back to back between the 2nd couple, men facing women.

8 Reel of Four (started by men giving the right shoulder to dancer opposite) finishing ready for Poussette.

8 Poussette.
1st couple repeat with 3rd couple.

British Grenadiers

Until the end of the eighteenth century every regiment had a contingent of grenadiers. These were soldiers who were picked for their height — an asset when they were throwing grenades. Grenades went out of use for a period during the nineteenth century and at that time the name was given to a company made up of the tallest men. In the British army today it survives in the First Regiment of Foot Guards — the Grenadier Guards — who are noted not only for their height and physique, but also for their discipline and ancient traditions.

Music: *The British Grenadiers*

Description
A longways set

4	Men advance and retire.
4	Women advance and retire.
4	1st couple cast off, each dancing down the outside of their own side to the bottom of the set.
4	1st couple dance up the centre of the set.
8	Six hands round and back.
8	1st and 2nd couples Poussette. Repeat until all are back in their original places.

Buchan Eightsome Reel

This dance is performed in two parts, the second part giving individuals a chance to show off their fancy footwork in the middle of the circle.

Music: *Any good reel*

Description
Four couples form a circle

Part 1

8   Eight hands round and back again.

8   Starting by giving the right hand to partner, Grand Chain halfway round.

8   Right hands across with women inside holding hands. Dance right round.

8   Giving right hand to partner, Grand Chain for the other half, reaching original places.

8   Left hands across, this time with men inside.

Part 2

8   1st woman goes inside the circle. She sets on her own while other dancers circle seven hands round and back.

8   1st woman sets to her partner and turns him with the right arm, hands gripping each other by the elbow. She then sets to opposite man and turns him with left arm also using elbow grip.

8   1st woman sets to man who was originally on her right and turns him with the left arm. She then sets to man who was originally on her left and turns him with the right arm.

8   1st woman dances Reel of Three with partner and opposite man, giving right shoulder to partner.

(continued on page 28)

Buchan Eightsome Reel
(continued from page 27)

8   1st woman dances Reel of Three with the other
     two men, starting with the man she turned first
     and giving him her left shoulder. As the Reel of
     Three finishes, she returns to her place and 2nd
     woman goes into the middle of the circle.
         Part 2 is repeated until all women have been
     in the centre of the circle. Then the men have
     their turn, starting with 1st man. When all dancers
     have been in the middle, Part 1 is danced once
     again.

Cadgers in the Canongate

Edinburgh's famous Canongate joins the High Street to form part of the Royal Mile. The element 'gate' in the name is an old Germanic word for road. The Canongate, therefore, was the road which the Augustinian canons took to the Abbey of Holyrood House. A cadger was a man who carried goods either strapped to his back or his pack-horse.

Music: *Cadgers in the Canongate*

Description
A longways set

8	1st woman dances a Reel of Three with 2nd and 3rd men. 1st man does the same with 2nd and 3rd women at the same time. The reel is begun by giving the right shoulder to 2nd dancers. 1st couple finish in their original positions.
8	1st couple Reel of Three on their own sides of the set.
4	1st couple join near hands, set to 2nd woman then dance round to face 2nd man.
4	1st couple set to 2nd man, then dance back to their original positions.
4	1st and 2nd couples set and, with right hands across, dance half round to change sides.
4	Repeat giving left hands across to return to original positions.
4	1st couple cross over giving right hands and cast off one place, dancing down behind the 2nd dancer on the opposite sides of the set.
4	1st couple turn each other with the left hand to finish in 2nd place on their own sides of the set.
8	2nd and 1st couples dance Rights and Lefts. Repeat with 3rd and 4th couples.

Captain Macdonald's Fancy

No one seems to know which Captain Macdonald is referred to here. And no one seems to know what his fancy was, either. Perhaps it was dancing!

Music: *Any good reel*

Description
A longways set

8	1st couple dance down the set and back.
8	2nd couple dance down the set and back.
4	Right hands across.
4	Left hands across
2	1st man and 1st woman turn their 1st corners with right hand.
2	1st couple turn each other with left hand.
4	1st couple turn their 2nd corners then each other, finishing in 2nd place.
	1st couple repeat the dance with 3rd couple.

Circassian Circle

This dance, which first became popular in the late nineteenth century, when it was also popular in England, has the dancers going round the room like the Dashing White Sergeant.

Music: *Circassian Circle*

Description

With women on their partner's right, couples stand in a circle round the room facing another couple, ready to dance clockwise or anti-clockwise. All start together

8	Rights and Lefts with couple opposite.
4	Set twice to partner.
4	Turn partner with both hands to finish facing opposite couple.
8	Ladies' Chain.
8	Poussette and repeat with next couple.

College Hornpipe

In Scots the word 'college' is synonymous with 'university'. Which university this dance was devised for is not known.

Music: *The College Hornpipe*

Description
A long set

8   Six hands round and back.

8   1st, 2nd and 3rd couples Promenade.

8   1st couple cross over, giving right hands, cast off one place behind the 2nd dancer on the opposite side of the set then cross over again giving left hands. They cast off once more on their own sides of the set, dancing behind the 3rd dancer before dancing up the middle of the set to finish facing 1st corners. 2nd couple have moved up.

4   1st couple set to 1st corners, turning on the 2nd step to face partner across the set. Set to partner and turn again to face 2nd corners.

4   1st couple set to 2nd corners, turning on the 2nd step to face partner up and down the set. 1st couple clap hands and turn into their own sides one place down the set.
1st couple repeat with the next two couples.

Corn Rigs

The word 'rigs' refers to strips of land which were looked after by a number of tenant farmers. The form of the dance may show the making of a corn dolly, a magic symbol made from the last sheaf of corn to ensure further good harvests. The tune for Corn Rigs is an old hornpipe which was given words by Burns.

Music: *Corn Rigs*

Description
Four couples form a longways set

8	1st man and 1st woman cast off, dancing down the set on their own sides behind the other dancers and then back up again.
8	1st man dances a figure of eight round 2nd woman and 2nd man. He gives 2nd woman his left shoulder and 2nd man his right shoulder. At the same time, 1st woman dances a figure of eight round 2nd man, giving him her right shoulder, and 2nd woman, giving her her left shoulder.
8	1st couple dance down and up the middle of the set.
8	Poussette.

Repeat with 3rd couple.

The Dashing White Sergeant

Henry Bishop, whose song 'Home Sweet Home' may still be known to a few, composed the tune for a theatrical lyric, 'The Dashing White Sergeant' in the 1820s. At the end of the nineteenth century, the tune was married to a dance called La Danse Florence, a mixture of threesome reels and a 'Swedish' progression, and the dance became known as the Dashing White Sergeant.

Music: *The Dashing White Sergeant*

Description

Sets of three arrange themselves facing another set of three in a circle round the dance floor. Each set is made up of a woman flanked by two men or a man flanked by two women who face a member of the opposite sex in the other set

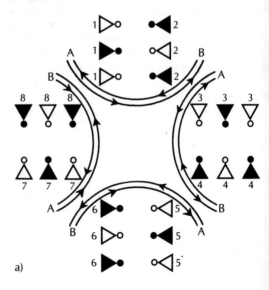

a)

8	Each set joins hands with facing set and dances six hands round and back (as in diagram a).
2	The centre dancer in each set sets to the dancer on his or her right and they turn.
2	The centre dancer now sets to the dancer on his or her left and they turn.
8	Each set performs a Reel of Three on its own side of the dance.
4	Dancers advance and retire, stamping their feet when they come closest to the opposite set.
4	Each set advances again, those dancing clockwise forming an arch so that the opposite set can pass underneath to face new dancers (as in diagram b).

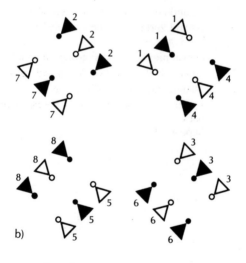

b)

Repeat from the beginning with each new set.
It is important that you always move in the direction you are facing at the start.

De'il Amang the Tailors

This was the name of a game played in public houses in the nineteenth century. It was played on a small board where nine small skittles were knocked down with a spinning top. The first player to knock down thirty-one skittles was the winner.

Music: *De'il Amang the Tailors*

Description
A longways set

2	1st and 2nd couples set to each other.
2	1st and 2nd couples change places, giving right hands across.
4	Repeat previous 4 bars, giving left hands across.
8	1st couple dance down the set and up again.
8	1st and 2nd couples Allemande.
8	Top three couples dance six hands round and back.

Repeat with 3rd couple.

The Duke of Perth

The Duke of Perth who gave his name to this reel was probably James Drummond, a staunch Jacobite, who was given the title by King James in 1695. This dance has the alternative titles Pease Strae and Broun's Reel.

Music: *The Duke of Perth*

Description
Sets of four couples facing each other down the room

8	1st couple turn each other with right hand, cast off one place on their own side (2nd couple moving up) and then turn each other 1½ times with the left hand, finishing facing 1st corner.
8	1st couple turn 1st corner with right hand, partner with left hand, 2nd corner with right hand and partner with left hand, finishing facing 1st corner.
8	1st couple set to 1st corner and turn with both hands, then set to 2nd corner and turn with both hands.
6	1st couple each dance Reel of Three with their corners, giving left shoulder to 1st corner to start.
2	1st couple cross back to own side in 2nd place ready to repeat with 3rd and 4th couples.

Eightsome Reel

The Eightsome Reel embodies one of the oldest ritual dance movements – dancing clockwise and anti-clockwise in a circle round a person or object. The dance was devised in the early 1870s by the Earl of Dunmore for the Atholl Gathering Ball. It has remained a popular dance ever since, though the Buchan Eightsome, which is a variation, is preferred by some dancers. Like the Buchan Eightsome it is performed in two parts.

Music: *Any good reel*

Description
Four couples make four sides of a square with
the women on their partners' right

Part 1

8	All four couples dance eight hands round and back.
4	Right hands across with women inside holding hands. Dance half round.
4	Left hands across with men inside. Dance half round.
4	Set twice to partner.
4	Turn partner with both hands.
16	Grand Chain.

Part 2

8	1st woman goes inside the circle and sets on her own while the other dancers circle seven hands round and back.
8	1st woman sets to her partner and they turn with the right arm, hands gripping the elbow; she then sets to the opposite man and turns with the left arm, also using elbow grip.

8   1st woman dances a Reel of Three with these two men, starting by giving the right shoulder to her partner.

8   1st woman sets alone in the middle of the circle while the others dance seven hands round and back.

8   1st woman sets to the man who was originally on her right and turns him with the right arm, elbow grip. She then sets to the man who was originally on her left and turns him with the left arm, once again using the elbow grip.

8   1st woman dances a Reel of Three with these two men, starting with the man she turned first and giving him her left shoulder. As the Reel of Three finishes, she returns to her place and the 2nd woman goes into the middle of the circle.

Part 2 is repeated until all women have been in the centre of the circle. Then the men have their turn, starting with 1st man. When all dancers have been in the middle, Part 1 is danced once again.

Flowers of Edinburgh

The tune, which first appeared in 1742, had the title 'My Love's Bonnie When She Smiles On Me'. The title and the words had been changed by 1751, possibly because the original words had too much of a Jacobite flavour about them.

Music: *The Flowers of Edinburgh*

Description
A longways set

2   1st woman casts off and dances down behind 2nd and 3rd women.

2   1st woman crosses over and dances up behind 3rd and 2nd men to partner's position.

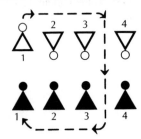

2   At the same time, 1st man follows, dancing behind 2nd and 3rd women and up the centre to partner's position.

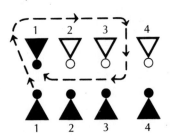

2	1st couple set to each other.
6	First 6 bars are repeated, this time with the man casting off and dancing down behind 2nd and 3rd women and his partner following. Both are now in their original positions.
6	1st couple set to each other.
8	Holding right hands, 1st couple dance down the set then up it in the centre.
8	1st and 2nd couples Poussette. 2nd couple take the place of the 1st couple in the line and vice versa.

Beginning in 2nd couple's place, 1st couple repeat above 32 bars, moving down one place every time until they reach the bottom of the set.

High Road to Wigton

Wigton in Dumfries and Galloway got its name from the Old English 'wic', a farm or settlement and 'tun', a homestead or farm. The name has now been anglicized to Wigtown.

Music: *Any good reel*

Description
A longways set

4   1st and 2nd women join hands to make an arch and dance across the set. 1st and 2nd men take hands and change places with their partners by passing underneath the arch.

4   1st and 2nd men join hands to make an arch and dance across the set. 1st and 2nd women take hands and pass underneath. Both couples are now back in their original positions.

8   1st and 2nd couples Rights and Lefts.

8   1st couple dance down and up the centre of the set.

8   1st and 2nd couples Poussette.
    1st couple are now in 2nd couple's position ready to dance the sequence again with the 3rd couple. When they repeat with the 4th couple, a new top couple begins.

Johnny Groat's House

John o' Groats is well known as being the most northerly village in Great Britain. Some centuries ago, three brothers by the name of de Groot came from Holland to the very northernmost tip of Caithness. They married local women and settled down, developing into a small community of eight families with the name o'Groat.

A story is told that one of them, John, angered by arguments about who should go into the dining-room first and take the top place at the table during a family gathering, built a house containing an eight-sided room with eight doors in which he placed an octagonal table. In this way, harmony was restored to the family.

Music: *Johnny Groat's House*

Description
A longways set

1st couple join both hands and dance down the middle and back up again using slip step.

1st couple cast off one place, dancing behind the 2nd dancer on their own sides of the set. They then meet in the middle, joining both hands. At the same time, 2nd couple move up.

1st couple repeat the above with couple three, finishing in 3rd place.

1st, 2nd and 3rd couples join hands and dance six hands round and back.

1st couple lead up to the top with four steps, set and cast off into 2nd place. At the same time, 3rd couple move down.

Repeat until everyone is back in their original positions.

The Lads of Saltcoats

James V established saltworks in Saltcoats in Strathclyde in the sixteenth century. The element 'coats' in the name refers to cottages which were built for the salt-pan workers.

Music: *The Lads of Saltcoats*

Description
A longways set

8	1st couple dance a Reel of Three with 2nd woman. The 1st woman begins the reel by dancing across the set, passing right shoulders with her partner.
8	1st couple dance a Reel of Three with 2nd man. 1st man beginning by dancing across the set.
6	1st couple dance down the set and back up again.
2	1st couple cast off, dancing down behind the second dancer on their own side into 2nd place. 2nd couple move up.
8	2nd and 1st couples Rights and Lefts.
	1st couple repeat the dance with 3rd couple. When they repeat with 4th couple, the next top couple begin.

Lord Eglinton's Reel

Music: *Any good reel*

Description
Four couples make a longways set

4   1st couple set once and cast off two places dancing down behind dancers two and three on their own sides of the set.

4   Repeat above, casting off up the set on the outside to return to original positions.

8   1st couple dance down the middle of the set and up again then cast off one place behind 2nd dancer on their own sides of the set. 2nd couple move up. 1st couple are now in 2nd place.

8   With the 2nd couple at the top of the set, 1st, 2nd and 3rd couples dance six hands round and back.

4   1st, 2nd and 3rd women join hands. 1st, 2nd and 3rd men do the same. All advance and retire.

4   All three couples turn partners with both hands. 1st couple repeat with 3rd and 4th couples.

Mairi's Wedding

Music: *Mairi's Wedding*

Description
A longways set

8   1st couple turn with the right hand and cast off one place, dancing down behind the 2nd dancer on their own side of the set. 2nd couple move up. 1st couple turn with the left hand to face their 1st corners.

4   1st couple dance half Reel of Four with 1st corners as follows: 1st woman passes 2nd man with the right shoulder while 1st man passes 3rd woman with the right shoulder. Having changed places, the corners stop dancing.

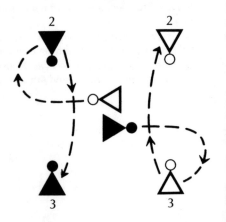

4   As soon as 1st couple have danced the above they move into the same formation with their 2nd corners, i.e., 1st woman passes 3rd man giving right shoulder while 1st man passes 2nd woman with the right shoulder so that these corners change places, too.

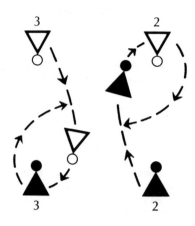

1st couple dance half Reel of Four with 1st corners again so that the corners return to their original positions.

1st couple dance half Reel of Four with 2nd corners so that they return to their original positions. *Note* If the above 16 bars are walked through before the dance, dancers will see that they are not as complicated as they look. The main thing to remember is that the 1st couple should always start off the half Reel of Four by dancing towards a member of the opposite sex. At the end of the formation couples 2 and 3 should be in their original positions.

All six dancers dance a Reel of Three across the dance, the 1st woman dancing with the 2nd couple and the 1st man with the 3rd couple giving left shoulder to 1st corner.

Six hands round and back.

Repeat.

Petronella

'Little Peter', danced to a hornpipe melody, has been popular in Scotland since the early nineteenth century

Music: *Petronella*

Description
A longways set

2   1st woman makes a ¾ turn to her right using a setting step to finish in the centre facing down the set. At the same time the 1st man does the same turning to his right.

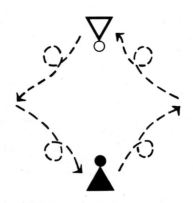

2   1st couple set to each other.
2   Repeat first 2 bars, each moving to the partner original position.
2   1st couple set to each other.
2   Repeat first 2 bars, so that the woman faces up the set and the man down the set.
2   1st couple set to each other.
2   Repeat first 2 bars to finish back in original positions.
2   1st couple set to each other once again.

1st couple, holding right hands, dance down the centre using a travelling step.

Still holding right hands, 1st couple dance up the centre with travelling step.

1st and 2nd couples Poussette.

1st couple repeat bars 1-32, always doing Poussette with the couple below them, until they reach the bottom of the set. Couples two, three and four repeat the whole of the above in turn until all dancers are back in their starting positions.

Quadrille Country Dance

Music: *Any good reel*

Description
A longways set

8 2nd man leads 1st woman down the set and back up again. On the last step he leaves her in his place beside 1st man and goes to stand beside 2nd woman who has moved up into first place. 1st woman is thus in 2nd position on her partner's right, opposite 2nd man. 2nd woman is in 1st position, on her partner's right, opposite 1st man.

8 1st and 2nd couples set twice. On their respective sides of the set, partners join both hands and turn once to finish, as they began, with 1st couple on the men's side of the set and 2nd couple on the women's side.

8 Ladies' Chain.

8 Poussette.
Repeat with next couple.

Reel of the 51st Division

Some of the men of the 51st Division who were captured during the Second World War at St Valéry were held in the German prisoner-of-war camp Laufen, where they devised a dance which they called the Laufen Reel. One of the men sent a copy of the dance's movements back to his wife in Scotland where the dance became well known as the St Valéry Reel. When the dance was published later it was given the name by which it is now known.

Music: *The Drunken Piper*

Description
A longways set

8   1st couple set, cast off two places, dancing behind the 2nd and 3rd dancers on their own sides of the set to meet below 3rd couple. They then join right hands and lead up to face 1st corners. 2nd couple move up.

4   1st couple set to 1st corner and turn with the right hand. Then, still holding right hands, 1st couple join left hands across the set to form a diagonal line.

2   All four dancers set in line.

2   1st couple turn each other with the left hand to face 2nd corners.

8   Repeat last 8 bars with 2nd corners then cross over to finish one place down in 2nd couple's position.

8   Six hands round and back.
     1st couple repeat with 3rd and 4th couples.

Twenty-First of September

A well-known date in the history of Scotland, 21 September 1745 saw the rout of Sir John Cope's army by the Jacobites led by Lord George Murray.

Music: *Any good reel*

Description
A longways set

8   1st couple lead off with 2nd and 3rd couples following, the women dancing down the outside of the set on their own side and round to the men's position. Men dance down the outside of the set on their own side and round to the women's position.

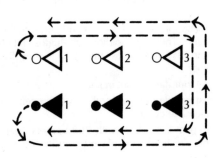

8   All three couples Allemande to the right so that the set now has the couples in the order, 3, 2, 1. The men are on the women's side of the set and vice versa.

8   Repeat first 8 bars, again with 1st couple leading off, so that everyone arrives on their own side but still in the formation 3, 2, 1.

3   All three couples Allemande to the left so that everyone arrives back in their original positions.

3   1st couple dance down the set and cast off at the bottom, the man dancing round behind 3rd man, in front of 2nd man and round into 2nd position, the woman dancing round behind 3rd woman, in front of 2nd woman and round into 2nd position.

1st couple repeat with 3rd and 4th couples.

The White Cockade

This Scottish tune was formerly called 'The Ranting Highlandman', before Burns turned it into a Jacobite song. The white rosette (cockade) was chosen as the emblem of the Jacobites in contrast to the black rosette favoured by the Hanoverians.

Music: *The White Cockade*

Description
A longways set

4	1st, 2nd and 3rd couples set and change places with their partners, giving right hands.
4	Repeat the above back to original positions.
8	1st couple dance down the middle of the set and back up again.
4	1st couple cast off one place, dancing down behind the 2nd dancer on their own side. 2nd couple move up.
4	1st and 3rd couples dance four hands round.
8	1st and 2nd couples Rights and Lefts.
	1st couple repeat with the next two couples.

JIGS

Berwick Johnnie

Music: *Any good jig*

Description
A longways set

2	1st and 2nd couples set once.
2	1st and 2nd couples dance right hands across half round.
4	Repeat the above 4 bars, dancing left hands across to get back to original positions.
8	1st couple dance down the set and up again, finishing ready for Allemande. 2nd couple come behind 1st couple on the last bar of the music.
8	1st and 2nd couples Allemande, 1st couple finishing in 2nd place facing 1st corners.
8	1st couple turn 1st corners with right hand, turn partner with left hand, turn 2nd corner with right hand and partner with left hand to cross over to own sides of the dance.
	Repeat with next couple.

The Frisky

Music: *Any good jig*

Description
A longways set

4	1st couple turn giving right hands and cast off, dancing behind the 2nd dancer on their own side into 2nd place. 2nd couple move up.
4	1st couple turn giving left hands and cast off, dancing behind the 3rd dancer on their own sides into 3rd place. 3rd couple move up.
8	Top three couples dance six hands round and back.
4	1st couple dance up to the top of the set. 2nd and 3rd couples move down.
4	1st and 2nd couples set twice.
8	1st and 2nd couples dance half Rights and Lefts, set on the opposite side of the set and cross over giving right hands so that the 1st couple are now in the 2nd couple's place. Repeat.

Hamilton House

Hamilton House was the palace of the dukes of the same name in Hamilton, not far from Glasgow. Not only was it a beautiful building, but it also contained some fine art treasures. Unfortunately, it had to be demolished in 1919 because of subsidence caused by coal mining beneath.

Music: *Hamilton House*

Description
A longways set

4   1st woman sets to 2nd man, turns 3rd man with both hands and stands between them.

4   1st man sets to 2nd woman, turns 3rd woman with both hands and finishes in line between 3rd couple facing up the set. At the same time, 1st woman moves into line between 2nd couple facing down the set, 2nd couple moving up.

4   Both lines join hands and set twice.

4   1st couple turn with both hands to finish with 1st man in line between 2nd and 3rd women, 1st woman in line between 2nd and 3rd men.

4   Both lines set twice.

4   1st couple turn to finish in 2nd place on their own sides of the set.

8   All three couples dance six hands round and back.
    Repeat with 2nd and 3rd couples.

Jessie's Hornpipe

Music: *Any good hornpipe*

Description
A longways set

8   1st man dances round 2nd man and 3rd man in a figure of eight. At the same time, 1st woman dances round 2nd and 3rd women also in a figure of eight.

8   1st couple dance down and up the set.

2   2nd couple join hands to make an arch and dance up the set. 1st couple join hands and dance under the arch into 2nd couple's place.

2   1st couple make an arch and dance up the set. 2nd couple join hands and dance under the arch back to their original positions.

4   Repeat the last 4 bars.

8   1st and 2nd couples Poussette.
      Repeat with 3rd couple.

Kiss Under the Stairs

Music: *Any good jig*

Description
A longways set

4	1st couple set and cast off one place, dancing down behind the 2nd dancers on their own sides to end up between 2nd and 3rd dancers.
4	1st and 3rd couples dance four hands round to the left.
4	1st couple set and cast off, dancing up behind the 2nd dancer and back to the top of the set.
4	1st and 2nd couples dance four hands round to the left.
4	1st couple dance down the set for two steps and up again in the middle.
4	1st couple cast off one place, dancing down behind the 2nd dancer on their own sides to meet in the middle of the set where they turn each other with the right hand.
4	1st man leads his partner between 3rd couple where they divide and cast off, dancing up behind the 3rd dancers and into 2nd place. The 2nd couple are now at the top of the set.
4	First three couples turn partners with the right hand. 1st couple repeat the dance with the 3rd and 4th couples.

Lamb Skinnet

The name comes from the German *Landsknecht*, a lance-bearing mercenary in the sixteenth and seventeenth centuries. There is also a German card game of the same name.

Music: *Any good jig*

Description
A longways set

4   1st couple set and cast off one place, dancing down behind the 2nd dancer on their own sides. 2nd couple move up.

4   1st couple dance half figure of eight round 2nd couple, finishing in 2nd place on the opposite sides of the dance.

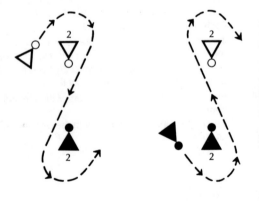

4   1st couple set and cast off one place, dancing down behind the 3rd dancer. 3rd couple move up.

4   1st couple dance half figure of eight round 3rd couple, finishing in 3rd place on their own sides of the dance.

8   1st couple dance up to the top of the set, set and cast off, dancing down behind the 2nd dancer on their own sides into 2nd place. 3rd couple move down.

8   2nd and 1st couples dance Rights and Lefts.
1st couple repeat the dance with 3rd and 4th couples.

Machine Without Horses

Many people mistakenly think the title of this dance refers to the invention of the steam locomotive. However, since both the dance and its tune were published in 1772, it may simply represent a horseless carriage.

Music: *Any good jig*

Description
A longways set

4	1st couple set and cast off one place, dancing down behind the 2nd dancer on their own sides. 2nd couple move up.
4	1st couple and 3rd couple dance right hands across.
4	1st couple set and cast off, dancing up behind the 2nd dancer on their own sides and back into their original positions.
4	1st and 2nd couple dance left hands across.
8	1st couple, followed by 2nd couple, dance down the set and between the 3rd couple. Dropping their partners' hands, the couples separate so that the 1st and 2nd women can dance round 3rd woman while the 1st and 2nd men dance round 3rd man. The 1st couple dance up to top and cast into 2nd position and the 2nd couple follow into 1st position.
8	1st and 2nd couple dance Rights and Lefts. 1st couple repeat with 3rd and 4th couples.

64

Off She Goes in the North

This jig originated in Aberdeenshire.

Music: *Any good jig*

Description
A longways set

8   1st woman casts off and dances down the set behind the 2nd woman, across the set and behind the 3rd man and across again behind the 4th woman. At the same time, the 1st man casts off, dances down the set behind the 2nd man, across and behind the 3rd woman and across and behind the 4th man.

8   1st couple retrace steps to original position.

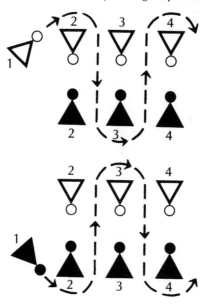

(continued on page 66)

65

Off She Goes in the North
(continued from page 65)

4	1st and 2nd men, and 3rd and 4th men, make arches and dance across the set, while 1st and 2nd women and 3rd and 4th women join near hands and dance together under their partners' arches.
4	Repeat the above with men again making the arches.
8	All couples Poussette, 2nd, 3rd and 4th couples all moving up one place, and 1st couple going straight to the bottom of the set.

The dance is repeated with a new top couple every time.

River Cree

The River Cree flows through Wigtownshire into Wigtown Bay.

Music: *Any good jig*

Description
A longways set

4   1st man and 2nd woman change places, giving right hands.

4   1st woman and 2nd man change places, giving right hands. Both sexes are now on opposite sides of the set with the 2nd couple at the top.

4   The two men join nearest hands and the two women join nearest hands. Advance and retire.

4   1st and 2nd couples return to their starting positions with half Rights and Lefts.

8   1st couple dance down the set and up again.

8   1st and 2nd couples Poussette.
     Repeat with 3rd couple and with 4th couple.

Strip the Willow

This is a weaving dance with the dancers mimicking the movements of the loom. Done throughout in running step, three steps to the bar, it is one of the simplest of the Scottish country dances though it is important to remember that your partner always receives your right hand and all the other dancers your left hand. Partners turn each other clockwise, other dancers anti-clockwise. The music is in 3 time, 2 bars to each turn.

Strip the Willow is a dance which encourages people to whirl and stamp in a way that many people would not call dancing at all.

Music: *Drops of Brandy*

Description
Four couples arrange themselves in a longways set

4	1st couple give right hands and turn each other 2½ times with the woman moving down. Her partner gets ready to turn her after she
2	Gives her left hand to 2nd man and turns with him.
2	1st woman gives right hand to partner. Both turn.
2	1st woman gives left hand to 3rd man. Both turn.
2	1st woman gives right hand to partner. Both turn.
2	1st woman gives left hand to 4th man. Both turn.
2	1st woman gives right hand to partner. Both turn.

Now it is the man's turn to dance with the women in the set.

12   Beginning with 4th woman, 1st man repeats his partner's movements all the way up the set, always turning his partner with the right hand.
1st couple are now back at the top of the set.

2   1st woman and 1st man give left hands to 2nd man and 2nd woman respectively and turn at the same time.

2   1st woman and man give right hands to each other and turn.

8   As above with 3rd and 4th couples.
1st couple remain at the bottom of the set and the whole is repeated by couples two, three and four until all are back in their original positions.

Waverley

Also called Fergus McIver, the title alludes to a scene in Sir Walter Scott's novel *Waverley* in which some important Jacobites, including the noble Fergus MacIvor, were tried and condemned to death.

Music: *Any good jig*

Description
A longways set

8	With the 1st woman leading, 1st, 2nd and 3rd women dance round behind the 1st, 2nd and 3rd men and back to their original positions.
8	1st, 2nd and 3rd men dance round behind the 1st, 2nd and 3rd women as above.
4	With the 1st couple facing down the set and 2nd couple facing up the set both couples set to the person opposite. Change places with the dancer opposite, giving the right hand.
4	As above, giving the left hand to return to original positions.
8	1st and 2nd couples Poussette with the 1st couple finishing back to back in the middle facing their own sides of the set ready for Double Triangles.
8	Double Triangles with 1st couple finishing facing the women's side of the set.
8	1st couple dance between 2nd and 3rd women and separate. The woman casts off up the set behind and round 2nd woman while the man casts off down the set behind and round 3rd woman to meet in the middle of the set once again. 1st couple cast off as before, this time dancing between the 2nd and 3rd men. They finish on their own sides of the dance one place down.

Repeat.

STRATHSPEYS

The Birks of Invermay

Invermay is a district in Perthshire where the River May joins the River Earn. Birks are birch trees.

Music: *The Birks of Invermay*

Description
A longways set

4   1st man and 2nd woman turn each other with both hands and return to places.

4   1st woman and 2nd man turn each other with both hands and return to places.

8   First three couples Promenade.

8   1st couple, giving right hands, cross over and cast off one place, dancing down behind the 2nd dancers on opposite sides of the set. They then lead up between 2nd couple, cross over to their own sides and cast off one place again, this time dancing behind the 2nd dancers on their own sides of the set. 2nd couple move up.

8   1st, 2nd and 3rd couple dance six hands round and back.
Repeat.

Ca' the Ewes to the Knowes

Burns set words to this Gaelic tune in 1787. The song tells of a shepherd boy courting a girl. (*Ca* – call; *knowes* – hillocks)

Music: *Ca' the Ewes*

Description
A longways set

4	1st couple cast off and dance down behind the dancers on their own sides to the foot of the set.
4	1st couple turn outwards and dance up behind their own sides to the top.
8	1st couple turn each other with the right hand then cast off one place, dancing behind the 2nd dancers on their own sides of the set. 1st woman dances round 2nd woman and 2nd man in a figure of eight, while 1st man dances round 2nd man and 2nd woman in a figure of eight to return to their original positions ready for Allemande.
8	1st and 2nd couples Allemande.
8	1st and 2nd couples Rights and Lefts.

1st couple repeats the dance with 3rd couple and with the 4th couple.

7

Glasgow Flourish

The coat of arms of the City of Glasgow reads 'Let Glasgow Flourish'.

Music: *Any good strathspey*

Description
A longways set

4	1st and 2nd couples right hands across.
4	1st and 2nd couples left hands across.
4	1st, 2nd and 3rd couples right hands across.
4	1st, 2nd and 3rd couples left hands across.
8	1st couple dance down and up the set to return to 2nd place. 2nd couple move up.
8	2nd couple dance down the set with others following. At the bottom of the set partners release each other's hands, women turning to the left and men turning to the right to dance back up to the top.

Repeat.

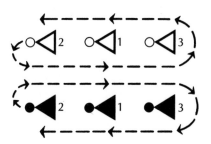

The Highland Plaid

Also called the Tartan Plaidie. A plaid used to be wrapped round the Highlandman's body as clothing during the day, to be taken off at night and used, if need be, as a blanket. This is what developed into a kilt. Nowadays, a plaid is a piece of tartan draped decoratively over the shoulder. The use of '-ie' as a diminutive is common in the north-east of Scotland.

Music: *The Tartan Plaidie*

Description
A longways set

4	1st and 2nd couples change places, giving right hands.
4	Repeat back to original positions.
4	1st and 2nd couples right hands across.
4	Repeat back to original positions with left hands across.
8	1st couple dance down the set and up again.
8	1st and 2nd couples Allemande.
	Repeat with 3rd couple.

Monymusk

Monymusk is in Aberdeenshire. The name comes from Gaelic and means 'a nasty peat bog'.

Music: *Sir Archibald Grant of Monymusk*

Description
A longways set

4	1st couple give right hands, turn and cast off one place, dancing down behind the 2nd dancer on their own sides of the set. 2nd couple move up.
4	1st couple give left hands and turn 1¼ times to finish with the 1st woman between 2nd couple, facing down the set and 1st man between 3rd couple, facing up. Each line of three joins hands.
4	All three couples set twice. On the 4th step 1st couple turn right to finish with 1st woman between 2nd and 3rd men and 1st man between 2nd and 3rd women in line with the other dancers in the set. Each line of three joins hands.
4	All three couples set twice.
8	1st, 2nd and 3rd couples join hands in a circle and dance four steps to the left and four steps back to the right.
6	1st man dances a Reel of Three with 2nd and 3rd women, beginning by giving his right shoulder to 2nd woman. At the same time 1st woman dances a Reel of Three with 2nd and 3rd men. She begins by giving her right shoulder to 3rd man.
2	1st couple cross over to their own sides of the set giving right hands in passing.
	1st couple repeat with next two couples.

Mrs Grant's Fancy

Music: *Any good strathspey*

Description
A longways set

8   1st man casts off, dances down behind the other men and back up again, while 1st woman does the same on her side.

8   With right hands joined, 1st couple dance down and up the centre of the set, finishing with 1st woman between 2nd couple (who have moved up) facing down, and 1st man between 3rd couple facing up.

8   All set twice, 1st couple turning into sidelines in 2nd place on their own side on 4th step. All set twice again.

8   1st three couples dance six hands round and back.
Repeat.

Sandy o'er the Lea

Music: *Any good strathspey*

Description
A longways set

8	1st and 2nd couples right hands across. 1st and 2nd couples left hands across.
8	1st and 2nd couples set and cross over giving right hands. Repeat back to place.
8	1st couple, followed by 2nd couple, dance down the middle and up again, the 2nd couple parting to let the 1st couple through.
8	1st and 2nd couple Allemande. Repeat with 3rd and 4th couples.

MARCH AND WALTZ

The Gay Gordons

The Gay Gordons is a couple dance in which pairs dance round the room. It is probably one of the best known and simplest of the dances done in Scotland. The original 'Gay Gordon' was Lord Strathaven, Fourth Earl of Aboyne (born 1761), a vigorous soldier. During a visit to France in 1783 he became very popular at the court of Louis XVI because of his gaiety and expertise at dancing.

Music: *Scotland the Brave*

Description

With women on their partner's right dancers make a circle round the room

Couples hold each other as follows: just as the dance is about to start, the man takes his partner's right hand in his right hand and her left hand in his left hand, so that their arms are crossed in front of them. He immediately lifts his partner's right arm over her head to a position just above her right shoulder. The man keeps his partner's left hand in his left hand at hip level so that he can lead her through the movement as follows:

2　Couples walk forward, anti-clockwise, for four steps.

2　Turn by the right, without dropping the grip, to walk backwards in an anti-clockwise direction for four steps, the left hands now joined over the left shoulder.

4　Repeat the above 4 bars walking in a clockwise direction.

4　Women turn underneath their partner's right arms while the men walk forwards.

4　Men take their partners in a waltz hold and polka.

Waltz Country Dance

This dance was first recorded in 1827.

Music: *Gowe o'er the Stream Charlie* and
Speed, Bonny Boat

Description
Stand in fours round the room, as in the diagram

8   Each man sets to woman opposite and crosses
to change places, passing right shoulder, women
making a waltz turn by the right and men moving
straight forward. Set to partners and again change
places.

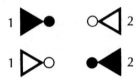

8   Repeat 1st 8 bars.
4   All four taking hands, balance forward and back-
ward.
4   Men continuing to balance on the spot, turn the
women on their left to the place on their right
(with both hands).
8   Repeat last 8 bars.
8   Poussette passing couple with whom they have
just danced to meet the next couple.
Note
Balance step used is like Pas de Basque omitting
4th beat.

DANCES FOR CHILDREN

As long as the figures are not too complicated even children can enjoy Scottish country dancing. The dances included here can also be danced by adults, of course.

Bonny Kitty

A reel with hand clapping which children like.

Music: *Any good reel*

Description
A longways set

8   1st and 2nd couples set twice, give right hands to their partners and cross over to the other side of the set. On the last two bars of the music all dancers clap three times.

8   1st and 2nd couples repeat above to return to their original places.

8   1st couple cross over between 2nd couple, dance behind 3rd couple and back up to the top of the set, crossing again between 2nd couple. 1st couple then cast off, dancing down behind the 2nd dancer on their sides into 2nd place. 2nd couple move up. All dancers clap three times.

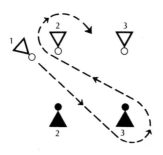

(continued on page 88)

87

Bonny Kitty
(continued from page 87)

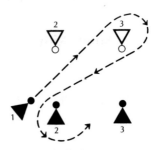

4	1st and 3rd couples dance four hands round to the left.
4	1st couple turn each other with the right hand and cast off, dancing behind and up the set on their own sides to their original positions. 2nd couple move down.
4	1st and 2nd couples half Rights and Lefts.
2	1st and 2nd couples give right hands and cross over to their own sides of the set. 1st couple are now in 2nd place on their own sides.
2	All dancers clap three times.

1st couple repeat the dance with the next two couples.

Campbell's Frolic

Music: *Any good jig*

Description
A longways set

2	1st and 2nd couples set.
4	1st and 2nd couples dance right hands across.
2	1st couple cast off, dancing behind the 2nd dancer on their own sides of the set into 2nd place. 2nd couple move up.
2	1st and 3rd couples set.
4	1st and 3rd couples dance left hands across.
2	1st couple cast off, dancing behind the 3rd dancer on their own sides of the set into 3rd place. 3rd couple move up.
8	1st couple set, join right hands and dance up the centre of the set to the top. 3rd couple move down so that 1st couple can cast off as before into 2nd place.
8	Top three couples dance six hands round and back. Repeat.

Cumberland Reel

A very nice jig in which the first couple dance through arches made by the other dancers.

Music: *The Cumberland Reel*

Description
A longways set

4   1st and 2nd couple dance right hands across.

4   1st and 2nd couple dance left hands across.

8   1st couple join hands and dance down the middle of the set and back up again.

6   1st couple followed by all the other dancers cast off, turning outwards from the set and dancing down on their own sides.

6   1st couple meet at the bottom of the set and lead the other dancers back up the middle to their original positions. On the last step the 1st couple join near hands and face down the set. All the other couples join hands with their partners to form arches.

4   1st couple dance under the arches to the bottom of the set. On the last step all the dancers drop hands.
A new top couple repeat the dance.

Kelso Races

Music: *Kelso Races*

Description
A longways set

8   1st boy and 2nd girl dance towards each other with two steps, dance back for two steps, then dance forwards again and with right shoulder to right shoulder pass closely back to back. Passing with left shoulder to left shoulder, dancers return to their original places dancing backwards.

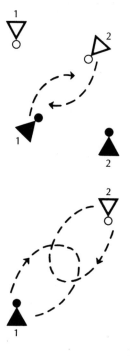

(continued on page 92)

Kelso Races
(continued from page 91)

8   1st girl and 2nd boy do the same.

8   1st couple cast off one place, dancing behind the 2nd dancer on their own sides of the set. They meet briefly in the middle of the set, separate and cast off up round and behind the 3rd couple and into 2nd place.

8   2nd, 1st and 3rd couples join hands in a wide circle. All advance and retire then drop hands so that all three couples can turn their partners with the right hand to return to their own sides of the dance.

Repeat with 3rd and 4th couples.

Soldier's Joy

This reel comes from the west of Scotland.

Music: *Soldier's Joy*

Description
A longways set

8	1st couple cast off, dancing down the outside of the set on their own sides behind the other dancers. They join hands at the bottom of the set and dance up the middle together to arrive back in their starting positions.
4	1st, 2nd and 3rd couples right hands across.
4	1st, 2nd and 3rd couples left hands across.
8	1st couple join hands and dance down the middle of the set and back up again.
8	1st and 2nd couple Poussette. Repeat with 3rd and 4th couples.

DANCE PROGRAMMES FOR SPECIAL OCCASIONS

In organizing a traditional dance evening several things should be taken into consideration.

The success of the dances depends on having enough space in which to do the formations properly, so the room or hall where the dance is being held should be big enough for the number of dancers.

For a four-hour programme sixteen to eighteen dances are needed. Programmes often include three extra dances, generally reels, to be done if there is time, but more often than not so many of the favourites are repeated that the programme is not danced through to the end. Most dances close with a slow waltz and 'Auld Lang Syne'.

The dances are done in groups of three – for example, one jig, one strathspey and one reel – with the pause between each dance being long enough only for the Master of Ceremonies to announce the next dance, the sets to form and the dancers to be talked through the formations if necessary. A longer pause between groups of three dances allows people to get a drink and have a chat before the next group of three starts. If a meal is to be served it is normally announced after the first six dances. After a meal it is advisable to restart the dancing with a slow waltz.

Live music, though it is best, is not always available so a selection of suitable records has been included at the end of this book.

Burns Supper

Robert Burns was born in Ayrshire on 25 January 1759 and this date is celebrated all over the world with Burns Suppers and dances. A traditional menu is served which includes haggis, mashed potatoes and turnip, and, of course, whisky.

After a guest of honour has recited Burns's 'To a Haggis', the haggis is brought into the dining-room accompanied by a piper. This is called 'piping in the haggis'. A ceremonial cut is made in the haggis with a sgian dhu (pronounced skee-an doo), the small knife which Scotsmen wear in the top of the hose, and then the meal begins. After the meal other poems are recited and speeches and toasts are made, particularly, because of Burns's love for them, a toast 'to the lassies', replied to by one of the 'lassies' present.

Programme
Machine Without Horses (jig)
Corn Rigs (reel)
Largo Law (strathspey)
Berwick Johnnie (jig)
Petronella (reel)
The Birks of Invermay (strathspey)

meal

Waltz Country Dance (waltz)
Glasgow Flourish (strathspey)
Admiral Nelson (reel)
Off She Goes in the North (jig)
Hamilton House (jig)
High Road to Wigton (reel)
Ca' the Ewes to the Knowes (strathspey)
Kiss Under the Stairs (jig)
The Duke of Perth (reel)
The Blithest Lass that Ever was Seen (strathspey)
Lamb Skinnet (jig)
Eightsome Reel (reel)
Sandy O'er the Lea (strathspey)

Last Waltz
Auld Lang Syne
* * *

Extras if time
Bonnie Geordie's Wig (reel)
College Hornpipe (reel)
Johnny Groat's House (reel)

St Andrew's Night

St Andrew is the patron saint of Scotland. He was crucified in Patrae in AD 70 on the *crux decussata*, the diagonal cross which is also used for the Scottish flag or Saltire. St Andrew's Day is 30 November. Though it is less frequently celebrated in Scotland nowadays, it is still regarded as an important date by expatriate Scots, many of whom belong to St Andrew's societies.

Programme
Waverley (jig)
The Cumberland Reel (jig)
The Highland Plaid (strathspey)

Cadgers in the Canongate (jig)
Flowers of Edinburgh (reel)
Glasgow Flourish (strathspey)

Jessie's Hornpipe (jig)
Circassian Circle (reel)
Monymusk (strathspey)

De'il Amang the Tailors (reel)
River Cree (jig)
Mrs Grant's Fancy (strathspey)

Campbell's Frolic (jig)
Buchan Eightsome Reel (reel)
Waltz Country Dance (waltz)

Lads of Saltcoats (reel)
The British Grenadiers (jig)
Largo Law (strathspey)

Last Waltz

Auld Lang Syne

* * *

Extras if time
The Dashing White Sergeant (reel)
Lord Eglinton's Reel (reel)
The Frisky (jig)

Hogmanay

Hogmanay is the last night of the year, a date when friends and relations meet to 'see in' the New Year with a party. Many old customs and superstitions are associated with this date. In Edinburgh, for example, the Hogmanay celebrations traditionally start at the Tron Kirk where the people begin to gather at about 11 p.m. ready to sing 'Auld Lang Syne' at midnight before going 'first footing', visiting friends. The 'First Foot', the first person to cross the threshold after midnight on Hogmanay, should be a tall, dark, handsome man carrying a gift of coal for luck. If the 'First Foot' is a woman, this can bring bad luck, especially if she has red hair.

The traditional foods offered at Hogmanay are black bun and shortbread and, of course, whisky.

Programme
The Gay Gordons (march)
The Duke of Perth (reel)
The Cumberland Reel (reel)

Campbell's Frolic (jig)
Flowers of Edinburgh (reel)
The Highland Plaid (strathspey)

Strip the Willow (jig)
Soldier's Joy (reel)
Monymusk (strathspey)

The Frisky (jig)
The White Cockade (reel)
Ca' the Ewes to the Knowes (strathspey)

Kelso Races (jig)
The Dashing White Sergeant (reel)
The Birks of Invermay (strathspey)

Machine Without Horses (jig)

De'il Amang the Tailors (reel)
Sandy O'er the Lea (strathspey)
Last Waltz
Auld Lang Syne
* * *
Extras if time

Hamilton House (jig)
High Road to Wigton (reel)
Eightsome Reel (reel)

Auld Lang Syne

This old song, which was embellished by Robert Burns, is probably the most famous song in the world. It is sung at the end of parties and dances and at the close of political rallies. Its use as a closing song dates from the early nineteenth century. For all that it is well known, many people do not know all the words. It is worth giving them here in full.

Should auld acquaintance be forgot,
And never brought to mind?
Should auld acquaintance be forgot,
And auld lang syne?

Chorus
For auld lang syne, my dear,
For auld lang syne;
We'll tak' a cup o' kindness yet,
For auld lang syne.

And surely ye'll be your pint-stoup,
And surely I'll be mine;
And we'll tak' a cup o' kindness yet
For auld lang syne.

Chorus

We twa ha'e run about the braes,
And pou'd the gowans fine;
But we've wandered mony a weary fit,
Sin' auld lang syne.

Chorus

We twa hae paidl'd in the burn,
Frae morning sun till dine;
But seas between us braid hae roar'd
Sin' auld lang syne.

Chorus

And there's a hand, my trusty fiere!
And gie's a hand o' thine!
And we'll tak' a richt gude-willie waught
For auld lang syne.

Chorus

stoup – jug; *gowans* – daises; *fiere* – friend; *a richt gude-willie waught* – a drink with right good will

Nowadays only the first verse, chorus and third verse are sung as a closing song. Everyone stands in a ring holding hands and sings verse one and chorus.

Many people want to start with the arms crossed but this is wrong. Only when verse five starts, with the words 'And there's a hand, my trusty fiere' are the hands released, the arms are crossed and the hands are re-clasped with the arms crossed. The arms are then shaken up and down as if shaking hands. Still with crossed arms the chorus is sung again and this time everyone walks or trots into the middle of the floor and back again.

Bibliography

The following books on Scottish country dancing are recommended.

Emmerson, George S., *Scotland Through Her Country Dances*, Galt House, Ontario, 1967

Hood, Evelyn M., *The Story of Scottish Country Dancing*, Collins, London, 1980

MacIntyre, Christine and Mina Corson, *Hop Scotch: Scottish Country Dancing for Schools*, the Royal Scottish Country Dance Society, Edinburgh

Pilling, F.L., *Scottish Country Dances in Diagrams*, 3rd ed, J.B. Elsey, Chester, 1969

Record List

Let's Dance, Ian Holmes and his Scottish Country
    Dance Band (cassette only LICS 5097). Include
    'The Duke of Perth', 'College Hornpipe' and
    'Eightsome Reel' as well as a set of strathspeys
    and a set of jigs.
Come Scottish Country Dancing, Robert Whitehead
    and the Danelaw Band (NRSCDS 105). Include
    'Corn Rigs', a hornpipe and several reels and
    jigs.
Music for Book 1 Dances, Bobby Crowe and his Scottish
    Dance Band (RSCDS 5). Includes 'Petronella'
    'Circassian Circle', 'Flowers of Edinburgh', 'Strip
    the Willow' and many others.
Music for Book 8 Dances, Jim MacLeod and his band
    (RSCDS 10). Includes 'The River Cree', 'Jessie'
    Hornpipe', 'Off She Goes in the North' and
    others.
The Dances and Dance Bands, (LILP 9003). Twenty
    tracks including 'Eightsome Reel'; 'Strip the
    Willow' and 'The Gay Gordons'.

The above records may be obtained from the Royal
Scottish Country Dance Society, 12 Coates Crescent
Edinburgh EH3 7AF.

Index to Dances